50 Easy Business Hacks

To Increase Your Sales

Thomas Rutledge

Introduction

Often, making a few changes or tweaks can make a whole lot of difference in the productivity of your business. Overnight, a business can swing from battling to survive to potentially big success by making the right changes in the right areas.

To help you achieve this, we have researched and considered 50 marketing and business practices and hacks got from high-ranked business and marketing experts from around the world. Hopefully, knowing how far we had to go may inspire you to apply some of these hacks to improve your business. The tips were compiled in an easy-to-read and easy-to-implement format, by giving a detailed explanation on each point, providing you with examples and ultimately giving you something to run with for each tip.

To achieve the best in your business, you need not apply all the tips at once. All it demands to achieve drastic change in your business may just involve applying a couple of these hacks at a particular time. Therefore, I beseech you to enjoy this book and start planning ways to inculcate some, if not all, of these 50 business hacks in your business!

1. Increase Your Charges

Often, business owners charge below what they should for the services they offer. Crank up your prices a bit, just to see the feedback you will get. Unfathomably, a higher priced commodity is often assumed to be of higher quality. Therefore, taking your price up can enhance good sales as it stirs people to come purchase your product or service. Consequently, charging more increases your profit margins because contrary to what you were making, this time you are making more per sale. Apply this strategy, take it a little further and focus your target on higher value clients.

Take for example, if you run a business coaching company and you get paid $200 per hour, take your price up to $1000. Eventually, this creates an assumption in the mind of the consumers that there must have been a boost in quality too. Hence, you can zoom in on establishments, companies or businesses that make a huge amount of money, against those that are hardly trying to stay afloat. Apparently, one new client will pay 5 times what the former client used to pay. Hence, you have boosted your rate per hour and reduced the equivalent amount of work required to earn that exact sum of money.

Something to run with: Take your prices up and narrow in on customers who can afford to pay more money for your products and services.

2 Separate Your Offers into Different Grades—Premium or Basic and charge the equivalent price for each.

Re-strategize and see what you can add to your product such that can make it worthy of being call a premium offer Also, you can consider how to package your offer such that it appears more "ready-made". After putting these in view, price your different packages effectively. Ensure to price the premium offer properly. The funny thing is that most prefer to go for the premium because the offer is more appealing and it is "ready-made" than just a service that may be a little bit tasking or demanding for the client. In addition, only a few people to offer premium service, so there's little or no competition.

Imagine a premium service of charging $497 to $997+ to write five articles, open a blog, post the articles on the blog, maximizing the use of keywords and have a good graphic design for the post instead of charging $5 to write one article. If you were to give the article to an outsider to write, paying $3 for $5 article, you only get to make a profit of $2. In addition, if you choose to write the article, about 30 minutes of your time would be spent on a $5 article and that is at top speed ($10 per hour). However, doing it the first way considered, the articles may be outsourced for $15. Another $10 could be set aside for great graphics on Fiverr.com and put in $25 to $50 to outsource the custom blog with SEO (blogger.com blogs, for example can be created in a manner of minutes). Hence, a raw cost of $50 to $100 for a $400 to $950 profit. On the other hand, if you were to do the work by yourself, approximately 3 to 5 hours of work will go into it. That puts you at a range of earning $100 to $200+ per hour. Put that in comparison to $10 per hour just selling $5 article, which is better?

Something to run with: Examine how you can make your offer premium or "ready-made" by adding more services or bundling your products together to give more value. This provides you with an opportunity to boost your prices substantially, with your premium pricing and your premium product being commensurate.

3 Let Your Prices Leave Some Cents Behind. End with A 7, .97, 5 Or .95

If your price tag is $10, for example, let try charging $9.97. Although you only dropped some few cents, people assume that it is cheaper. This trick also works even on high priced items. For example, you may have never seen a car being sold for $30,000; instead, you see cars being advertised for $29,995.

Surprisingly, some people often go away thinking that the car mentioned in the example above, was for $29,000 in their mind (although they are able to clearly comprehend that the car is $30,000)

In recent years, plenty marketers have adoption this system of dropping some cents which implied that they ended their prices in 9 or .9; however, there is a new trend of ending prices in 7, .97, 5, or.95. Unwittingly, costumers by default think that this is less expensive. I know it's crazy, it has been working and it can work for you too. Hardly will you miss the chipped off cents after increasing conversions.

Something to run with: regulate your charges to end in 7, .97, 5, or .95 to present your prices cheaper and helps increase conversions.

4 Put Time Limit on Your Deals

Put time limit on your deals. Of which those that do not last more than a few days should have time limit on them. If you possess an e-mail list of customers, ensure to send them mails on the last day of sales to remind them of the deadline. Surprisingly, most sales will come on the final day! Owning a countdown timer is a persuasive to show that you are not joking! In furniture stores, end of the week sales is a thing often practices. This idea is similar to such practice. Although it is apparent that next week or two, there will be another sale, there is a likelihood of buying it now for the customer, once they catch wind that there's a sale on the service. Because of the bad habit of procrastination, applying deals with limited time can get people off their seats on their way to the store.

Let's imagine this, if you run a gym and decide to put a sale on gym membership, with terms that promise discount on the total price for people that sign up over the next three days or a certain number of one-on-one training sessions as a bonus. The three-day time limit produces a sense of urgency, compelling people to buy. Especially people that may have wanted to buy but have been procrastinating.

Something to run with: Create a time dependent deal, which is a kind of deal that people only get to take up within a particular time frame. The deadline creates a sense of urgency persuading people to buy. Remember to often remind your customers on your email list about the deadline. As observed, the largest sales will be made on the last day.

5 Put the Word "Only" before a Price

The way we describe items and the vocabulary applied during description influences how we later process these items in our minds. Take for example, "I matched a nail but there was only little blood everywhere" and "I matched a nail and there was blood everywhere," project two different pictures. Just as observed in the example above, the words applied in describing your charge makes a total difference to your sales. Considering something as, seemingly inconsequential a using the word "only" to qualify your charge can boost sales.

Let's consider this example: if the price point for a product or service of yours is $97, rather than writing just "$97", write "Only $97". By qualifying the price point with 'only', psychologically, you are projecting the price to be little. Hence you imply that the price is not that high also and that the deal is a good one, in comparison to the deal you would get anywhere else.

Something to run with: Apply the word "only" before your charges (e.g. "Only $97" not "$97"). Unwittingly, it psychological affects the people to think the value being gotten is greater than the amount being paid.

6. Mention a discount next to a Price Point

It is germane to make it known to customers when they are being given a discount or savings. This calls their attention to the fact that they're being given a great deal for more value. Psychologically, a discount suggests that we are getting a better deal which increases the chance of buying. Therefore, seeing a discounted item is a does not only persuade us to buy it now but it also persuades users that may never have considered the product to buy.

For example, when creating your price list, you might write: "$97 --- 50% Off Today! Seeing this, people assume they are getting a great deal which helps them justify the purchase and for newbies, is most likely to push them to buy.

Something to run with: Display a savings amount or percentage discount next to a price (e.g. $97 — 50% Off Today!). This makes customers assume that they are being presented with a great deal and can persuade customers that have not bought before or considered buying to buy.

7. Place Your Normal Price and Your Sales Price Side by Side

When the difference between your normal prices and your sales price is presented before your customers, it affects their decision to purchase. Setting up the normal price against the sales price suggests that the deal they are being presented with is great, getting all that value at a price that is lesser than the normal. Everyone love to think they are being given a bargain and by presenting both your normal and sale price side by side, it emphasizes the worth or value that they getting for money.

For example, when you set up a price list, write your prices as "Normally $197-Only $97 Today!"

Something to run with: In marketing, everybody wants a bargain. Create the mirage of a great deal by putting your "normal" price against your sales price. (For example, normally $197 — Only $97 Today!)

8. Provide a List of Differently Priced Up-sells

Up-selling is offering a complimentary or more developed version of a product or service that a customer is purchasing. A perfect example of an up-sell can be observed when you approach a local fast food joint, "would you like fries with that?' Even up-sells that are not so great can boost your revenue stream with 33% or more. Some up-sells can even boost your initial sales by a 100%. Hence, an up-sell is a productive way to boost the total value of a sale.

For example, if you have a dance school and one class is $15, you could employ the use of up-sells. Provision of 3 different up-sells with varying amount could be offered.

Up-sell 1-4 week course for $50

Up-sell 2- Gold membership: for $120 per month, there is liberty to attend as many classes as you desire.

Up-sell 3 - Pro dance package which goes for $200 a month, it provides you with the opportunity to attend as many classes and receive private tutorship for a month.

Something to run with: Present a range of up-sells at different prices to your costumers to boost the total revenue on each sale. Up-sells are complimentary or better offers of a service that is being purchased by a customer already.

9. Get into Partnership with Other Business

Consider partnering with others such that both of you could make profits off of each other but not a business that directly competes with yours.

For example, if you sell homemade candles, reach out to boutiques and find out if they would be interested in selling your candles (the boutique may not be buying the candles from you but they may just share in the sales with you). Also if you sell a social media management or SEO service, get in touch with firms that handle web designs that might not offer your peculiar service to their customers but offer them a good sales cut. In addition, offer to do all the work, support, etc. for their customers and the website company must market it as their own thing (a win-win for both parties). From another view, if you are a programmer or have a tool of your own, reach out to the top companies in the market in your industry who might be able to sell your product and sell it as their own for a good share of the profits while you maintain it and do support for it. Getting one good deal here can be worth more than just having your own stand-alone business.

Something to run with: Find other business partner who are not necessarily in competition with you and partner with them. Take time to evaluate how you could have a win-win situation from them selling your product; whether it's by sharing sales, meeting a need that they do not offer but their clients have and permitting them to sell your service as their own or white labeling your product for their clients.

10 Recognize what Your Competition is Doing Right and See How You can apply it

Take time off making research concerning where your competitors advertise, spy on their sales funnel and how you can apply any good idea that you come across that appears to be working well, in your own business. Online, there are many tools that can help you discover what adverts and keywords your competition are employing. In addition, there are a couple of basic ways to see what your competitors are undergoing—follow them on social media, subscribe to their blogs, newsletters and channels. If they sell their items at smaller prices, you may have to purchase their product, to see what their process of purchase is like, find out if the offer upsells or not, what the upsells are and how the process that they put in place to follow up sales works.

For example, if you sign up to a competitor's new letter, you can get insight into how they nurture a business lead and turn it into actual sales. Eventually, you learn these tips and ask yourself: is it applicable to my own business?

Another way is to purchase a small item from them, find out if they are offering upsells and terms of the upsells, leaving you to consider if you can apply that to your business.

Something to run with: Discover where and how your competitors advertise and what their sales funnels are. Examine what they are doing well and consider how you can replicate this for your business.

11. Do Not Wait for Lead to Come to You; Go Meet the Leads

Building a sign-up page and waiting for leads to sign-up or reach out to you or waiting for potential leads to find your store and purchase your products or service may not be good enough to boost your business. Rather, it may demand that you actively go out and seek prospects.

Pay attention to the question that are being asked, that are relevant to what your business offers, on forums, Q&A sites (like Yahoo Answers) and social media such as Facebook, Twitter and Instagram.

Once you find this question, take a minute to answer these questions, ascertain that you provide value most importantly. This helps you gain extra following for your business, positions you as an authority in your niche. Taking advantage of this edge, you can start to build trust between you and potential customers and may get you some sales.

For example, if you have a business that renders SEO services, look for questions that pertain to best way of website optimization. Once you find these questions, you can proceed to answering such questions. You could leave an answer like. "Here are three tips that I find most effective: (insert your tips). If you need more information, I assist people with the SEO, by providing information and handling it all for them and here is a link to an article I wrote, itemizing seventeen tested way to step up your search engine optimization." Unknowingly, you have already provided great information and immense value in your response; persuasive enough, to make people click the links leading to your site.

Something to run with: Go in search for leads rather than waiting for leads to come. Join forums, check Q&A sites (like Yahoo Answers) and social media (Facebook, Twitter, Instagram) to find questions being asked that are in line with what you offer. Endeavor to answer the questions, providing good value, to boost your exposure and make likely sales.

12 Join Facebook Groups that are Relevant to your Niche and See What People Are Complaining About!

Seek out Facebook group that are relevant to your niche, join them and take time to read through, observing what people are complaining about. Then, begin to ask yourself the important questions, what are the common complaints that keep coming up over and over again? What product or service could you give that would provide a lasting solution to these complaints? Immediately you find these solutions, sell it or preferably, making it available for free to build followers.

For example, if you run an event planning business with wedding planning as your niche, join Facebook groups that focus on that niche and see what brides-to-be often complain about. Perhaps they find it burdensome and overwhelming to call to mind everything to put in place, and knowing when a particular thing should be done. You could take advantage of this and could create a timeline checklist, of what to put in place and when to put it in place as they countdown to the big day, and offer it for free to build a list of potential clients.

Something to go run with: Join Facebook groups within your niche and observe what people complain about the most. Provide a solution for these complaints. After that, decide to either sell it or use it to build a network of followers by giving it out for free.

13. Use Testimonies of Satisfied Customers as a Selling Point

Social proof is a great weapon for advertise your product. The testimony of a satisfied customer can become an effective way of talking about your offer than you talking about yourself. To make your marketing strategy less mechanical but quite flexible and relatable to customers is to include case studies from other customers who have consumed your products and services

For example, rather than talking about why people need to buy your SEO service, write an article, blog post or Facebook post talking about how a business went from bad rankings to #1 rankings and had more sales in under two weeks with a handful of easy tweaks...and then focus on the process and how the services you provided enhanced such growth. Most times, the response to such a post is that a number of people will naturally gravitate towards reaching out to you, to have you replicate such in their own situation.

Something to run with: Use case studio to talk about your service or product and the commensurate results that it gave your customers. Engage the people through articles, blog posts or Facebook posts.

14 Give Something of Value Away (And Monetize the Back-end)

Everybody loves a freebie! Everybody loves getting things for free. What do you currently sell that has value that could be offered to costumers for free? How can you monetize what comes as a result of this freebie—back-end? This is most effective if you can offer something other business would normally monetize.

For example, if you have a corporate cleaning business, you could offer the first cleaning free, and follow up with the customer, to inquire if they were satisfied with your services and would like to have you continue. This is a quite effective way to get new client to have a taste of your service, as you're taking the responsibility of bearing any risk from them and if the job you did is great, there is a high probability that they would want you to keep on. Unknown to them, you have activated the principle of reciprocity, which means that you've given something of value and the odds are they'll feel a compulsion—an urge—to do the same.

Something to run with: Assess yourself and find something of value that you can give away and then look at how the back-end can be monetized. Be it a sample of your service or a physical product, this is most effective if it is something normally charged for.

15. Make Your Service a Bundle to Create a "Package Deal"

Consider how you can make your service or product come together in a bundle to create a package deal. This may act as a great way to move more products and services, even to the public spectacle. Customers feel it's a great deal because, according to them, they are paying less for a bundle—which is a compendium of services—than they would have paid for each service separately. However, you get the benefit of a higher dollar sale per transaction. Bundling can also help you push slow-moving products and provide you an uphill to offer customers that may have been seeking to purchase just an individual item.

For example, if you run a travel agency, offer a package deal where accommodation, flights, several meals and a side attraction are included. Another example, if you own a beauty salon, provides a pampering package, where a hair styling, manicure and massage are offered together. Although a customer may have come with a plan to purchase one or two of these items, if you offer a really great deal, they may be persuaded to purchase the while package.

Something to run with: Bundle several of your services or products together to create a package deal. This offers something new for your customers, which gives great value and provides you with a platform to upsell, push slow-moving products and boost your dollar value per sale.

16. Provide Complimentary Offers for Your Current Customers

Realistically, it is a whole lot easier to sell to your current customers than to get one new customer. Based on the trust that had been built over time because of the efficacy of your product and your interaction with customers, they have grown to trust you. Take advantage of that trust by looking at what else you can sell to them that compliments what they bought previously.

For example, if you have a resume writing service, you could go all out for recent customers and offer an additional service where you submit their resume to a specific amount of job adverts and write a cover letter customized for the purpose of each specific advert and also submit their resume to several recruitment agencies.

Something to run with: Selling to your current customers is a lost easier and more cost effective than trying to obtain a new customer. Reach out to your current and past customers with a complimentary offer to what they have brought from you in the past. It's also a way of appreciating them.

17. Request Referrals from Your Customers.

Have you ever purchased a product or service because a friend, colleague or family member told you to give it a try? Apparently, we all have, at one time or the other because we trust that person and we take their recommendation more seriously over that of someone we barely know. This is the power of referrals. Ask your customers if they have friends, family or people them know that may love your service, and then reach out to those people on their behalf, offering your services and products.

For example, imagine you have an e-commerce business where you deal in natural beauty products. You could send out emails to your customer list, asking them if they have anyone who would love your products as much as they do. If they have anyone like that, ask them to pass the email address of such people to you. Also add that you would offer their friend a free sample of your best products while they—the current customers—will receive a 15% bonus off the next purchase they make online as an appreciation. When you send the email to the new lead, advertising your products and services, mention that their friend thought they would like your product and services, which is why you sent the e-mail and would love to offer them a free sample as a gift.

Something to run with: Get to work immediately and begin to send those mails to your customers asking if they know people that they think would love your products/services and if they would be of utmost help to pass the contact information of such people on to you. When the mail is sent in, reach out to those people, mentioning how you got their contact information and cut them a special offer.

18 Provide a Loyalty Package

A loyalty package is an effective way to persuade customers to keep buying from you, make them feel special by rewarding them and thanking them for the continued patronage. Normally, loyalty packages involve rewarding customers for buying from you regularly or for purchasing a certain amount of goods from you, whether it's in free product or discounted future purchases.

For example, imagine that you own a local coffee shop. Many local coffee shops implement a simple punch-card royalty program. With these cards, you are allowed to purchase 5 coffees and receive a 6th coffee on the house. This well-crafted reward plan encourages people to keep coming back to that same coffee place to get a daily those of their caffeine supply.

Something to run with: Set a loyalty program that rewards customers that meet the terms of the program. Reward such customers through free products/services or discounts for future purposes.

19 Employing Future-Use Coupons

When customers purchase products or services from you, give then a coupon for the value of a dollar or a percentage off their next purchase. This is called "future-use" coupon. This is to encourage your customers to come back and make more purchases from you again and to keep you in mind. Receiving the coupon could even be made dependent on spending a certain amount, to encourage customers to spend more per sale.

For example, if you own a tennis shop, you could implement an offer in which for every over $100 spent a day in the shop, the customer gets $15 off their next purchase of $100 or more. Serving as an incentive for your customer to spend $100 now, it also gets you an additional $100 sale next time they come in to use their coupon.

Something to run with: Persuade customers to come back to your store with "future-use" coupons. Explain the terms to them and let them know that for spending a particular amount today, they get a percentage off or dollar discount for the next time they come to make a purchase with you.

20. Membership Program

There should be a provision for your customers to sign up, either for free or for a small amount, to be part of a community or an elite club. This is called a membership program. To persuade people to sign up, they often receive special discounts, invitations to product launching events, early access to the product and other rewards. The advantage of running a membership program is that by offering these rewards to loyal customers, you encourage them to keep purchasing from you. Another added benefit is that you may begin to build a list of clients, from these loyal ones, that you can regularly market to and offer deals to.

For example, if you run an online store and you sell healthy food products, creating a VIP membership plan for customers with one of its benefit being free shipping is a good idea. Special deals such as a free gift (perhaps a sample of new product that you want to promote) with each purchase over $30 could be offered. In addition, the free shipping encourages people to join your VIP Membership Plan, providing you the avenue to continue marketing to them regularly and the free-gift-with-purchase offer encourage them to purchase from you.

Something to run with: Implement a membership program, invite your customers to become a part of a community and receive special benefits (e.g. free shipping, early access to sales, special deals, free gifts with purchase) from you. This provides you with endless advantages like the platform to build a list of leads and customers to market to. In addition, owing to these benefits, customers continue to purchase the product or service from you.

21 For Certain Amount Spent, Give a Gift

To encourage people to come buy from you, offering a gift for a purchase made, over a certain amount is quite effective. In addition, considering the gift might encourage people to spend more per sale. It even works better when the free gift is a sample of another product that you want to promote. In fact, it may even be a new product that you want to customers to give a try so as to make more sales on the product.

For example, brands that deal in beauty products employ this strategy quite often and it works greatly! These brands offer a selection of beauty products. Each product is not as large in quantity as the one to be sold—more like a trial version. These products are put in attractive cases and given out as gifts for purchases over $50, $70, $100 in one transaction. Beyond encouraging their customers to buy more products in one transaction, it provides a platform to introduce their customers to new products that they may not have noticed, if they had not gotten the opportunity to try it once.

Something to run with: Within your store and your wide range of products, look at what you may offer as a free gift to customers when they spend over a certain amount of money in one transaction. Eventually, your customer spends more per sale and they also get an opportunity to try new products, if those products are your gift.

22 Offer a Guarantee on Your Products or Services

Presenting your customers with a guarantee is an effective way to encourage them to buy from you. For the customers, it's delightful to be able to get an easy way out of purchasing a product if you discover within the accepted period that you do not like it. It takes the risk of loss off the customer. Psychologically, it helps them build confidence in your product—I mean, why would you offer a guarantee if you were not confident in your product? Essentially, do not whack an awesome guarantee on a product that is not great. Ensure that your products or services are great.

For example, if you run a mattress company, you could offer a guarantee and present it like this: "Try our mattress without risk for 30 days. If it turns out that you are dissatisfied with the mattress we will make a 100% refund." Such a guarantee as this takes out the risk of buying for your customers and builds a confidence in your product. Often people would not make use of the guarantee—this result also largely depends on how good your services are. Hence the amount of returns you would make against the increase in sales would be very worth it.

Something to run with: To your customers, offer a guarantee that takes the risk out of the purchase for the customer. However, ensure that whatever product you are selling is really of good quality that you can stand for anytime. Ensure that your guarantee is made obvious. Most importantly, ensure that those extra sales should far outweigh the people that you have to pay back from the guarantee.

23. Pay Attention to The Benefit of Your Products and Services.

In whatever marketing strategy you employ, do well to keep your focus on the how advantageous your products and services are to the customers instead of just focusing on their features. The advantages, benefits and the need that your products and services meet are what sell it not the features. For example, a person who buys an anti-aging cream would want to be sure that the ingredient Q10 is contained in it or that it obviously reduces wrinkles and makes them look years younger. Come up with a way to use the benefits of your products provide in marketing your products. In fact, you can still use the features, but not in isolation. However link the advantages to the feature and present it before the customer.

For example, if you have a business that deals in selling a course material that handles guitar teaching lesson, you may have three main features that could evolved into benefits for your students.

Feature 1: Over 50 pages of guitar lessons

Benefit 1: Learn to play the guitar under 3 hours.

Feature 2: Training on how songs are composed

Benefit 2: After this class, you will be able to create your own songs.

Feature 3: Practice how to play over a dozen songs with stepwise instructions to help you through.

Benefit 3: At the end of this session, you will be able to play over a dozen great songs in no time!

From the example above, every time you mention the feature, what the students is to gain out of it must follow, explaining what the feature is supposed to ultimately achieve in the student.

Something to run with: Examine your strategies and examine how you can accentuate the benefits that the customer enjoys from your services as opposed to focusing only on the features. The features are still very much important, especially in certain products but ensure to link the features to what the customers would enjoy out of that feature. Therefore you may need to ask yourself a question quite often: what is in it for the customers to gain?

24 Request For feedback From Your Customers

Encourage your customers to give you a feedback, so you may know the common view of your product. These feedbacks often answer the questions: What do my customer like most about my product? How can I pay attention to what they like most, in my market? What do the customers believe your product lack? How can I use their feedback to create a highly improved service and offer to my customers?

For example, if you run a website creating business and the common feedback that you get from you customers is that they desire that you help rank their site on search engines. This may be added as an additional service, such that for a certain monthly token, you help rank their website. However if this service happens to be something you have no knowledge in, you could outsource it but white label as your own service. Ultimately, you make your profit on that service but need not do any work. To position yourself as a listening service producers, you can offer this service to your current customers, informing thy due to their helpful feedback and their demand, you have put in place a service to provide that service which they want.

Something to run with: Request for feedback from your customers, on what they enjoy the most and what they the like the least amidst your offered services. Take the feedback to the drawing board and use it to highlight what they like the most and keep making it better. Also, what they claim to like the least, look into it if there is a way to improve it and make it better, so you can offer your customer the best.

25 Offer Free Trials or Product Demonstration

Sometimes, it's difficult to envision the advantage of something that we have not seen being used before or seen in use before. Therefore offering a free trial or a product demonstration can be a plausible way to alleviate the fears that may arise in heart of a customer or potential customer's fears over the potency of the product. Instead, it makes the customer confident that the product will function for them. From another view, anytime someone tries something from you for free, they feel obligated to reciprocate by buying that product from you. It's the principle of reciprocity at work.

For example, a software company, offers a free 30 day trial so that customers can understood, see how the software works, use it and see if it gives the results they—the software company—get from it. This is inviting to customers who may have delayed, and remained indecisive to come and purchase because they can get the tip of an iceberg—a firsthand experience—of how good the product functions.

Something to run with: Let customers find it easy to see and locate the value in your product and purchase by giving a free trial period or product demonstration. To your advantage, the chance to make your customer feel comfortable with your product is provided for you and an opportunity to be how great it will work for them before they have to give their money. This hack leads to more tide-changing sales, considering that some people who may have had bias concerning your product with the chance to try it first may change their mind.

26 Within a certain Time Frame, Offer Free Shipping or Reduce its Cost

It is distasteful to have been searching for a particular item for a long time and to eventually find it at an amazing price then see that the shipping is going to cost you a fortune. To increase your sale over a short period of time, you may need to consider reducing the cost of your shipping or offer free shipping for a short period. By adding a time limit, a sense of urgency is unconsciously put to work in the head of the people, encouraging customers to come buy it now as another day may be too late. It is also a great way to encourage customers who may have doubts in buying from you to make a purchase now!

For instance, if you have business that sells supplies for gardening online, you can offer a promo telling your customers that for any supplies ordered by midnight on Sunday, you will deliver the supplies free. For cases of regular customers who purchase from you in large quantities, you may call them one on one giving them this information. Make it obvious on your website that you have this offer available only for a limited time—it may just be displayed as the first thing on your website.

Something to run with: For a short period of time, offer free shipping or reduced cost of shipping on products. This short time frame presents your offer as urgent, stirring customers to make their purchase now, not at a later date and encourages the indecisive ones to make a purchase—I mean, the shipping is free!

27 Put a Theme to Your Promotions (Seasonal, Holiday)

Promotions do a great work in helping to drive sales, especially for those who are not decisive to know whether they want to buy from you or not. In this next point is a tweak that may even help more in your promotions. Offering a seasonal or holiday themes promotions can help to drive sales faster because prospects understand by the season or holiday being celebrated that the offer is for a limited time. However never forget that to hit customers up at the peak of the buying period and on about a day to the last day of the promotion.

For example, a number of people are already buying stuff over Christmas, Valentine's Day, and Black Friday. You can take advantage of these periods by providing a special service or product that customers may perceive as unique and special—a service that is able to take their gaze off your competitors.

Like other promotions, it is advisable to keep these promotions within a very limited time (although the promotion may keep showing up intermittently) in order to prevent potential or indecisive customers from delaying too long. Therefore, offer a deal, keeping it within three or so days which are the perfect amount of time to offer a special promotion deal. Just ensure to give them as man reminders as possible as the time goes on. For instance, if you have an email list, mailing them once on day one, twice on day two and three times on day three. This technique will get you a lot of sales on the last, especially at the eleventh hour, when there's no time left.

Something to run with: During holidays or at different seasons of the year or any other special time, it is a productive idea to invent themed

31

promotions with special promotions to drive extra sales and, even more to also stand out from the other competitors during a period of high sales.

28 Send a "We Haven't Seen You in a While" With a Thank You and an Incentive

Being caught up in trying to makes sales, most businesses tend to ignore their prospects and their clients. For your sales, this is a horrible thing to do, as you would be losing a ton of money by this wrong decision.

To remind your prospects and customer about you, trying sending them am email or a card with something like a note of appreciation accompanied by an incentive that may stir them to come purchase products or services from you (a discount or a freebie that may lead them to come enjoy a sale offer from you).

For instance, if you have potential clients that have not bought from you yet but have expressed an interest in buying from you, you may choose to reach out to them automatically (via an auto responder) or following them up manually by writing an email directly, saying how you have not heard from them in a while. In addition, thank them for reaching out to you in the past, then let them know about a freebie that you want to offer them, which can eventually lead into a paid offer, or a discount or other deals that you currently have. Such an approach can help revive old these leads into being active buyers.

Also, if you have an existing client that has become inactive since, reaching out to them with a thank you for being a customer along with an offer—a freebie or special offer exclusively for customers—can be a great way to make a lot of sales without so much effort.

Something to run with: Reach out to old leads and inactive customers with a message that can be summarized as "we have not seen you in a while", a thank you note alongside a freebie, an incentive or discount assist in driving more sales from them towards you also making them feel appreciated at the same time.

29 Begin an Affiliated Program

Do you desire a way to make sale without paying for any advert and with no risk of losing money doing so? If your answer is "yes" then this is the way. Most business owners do not actually know the advantages of running their own affiliate program so they do not count it important.

Affiliate programs are the platform where you offer others a small cut of any sale that you get by referrals from them. Doing this online, there are special "affiliate links" that you send to them. When they refer people to you through those links and those people eventually buy from your site, they would get paid a percentage of the sale. This process can also work offline by letting other people or customers refer your prospects. In return, you manually credit then. An alternative technique is to give out specific coupon codes to other people or customers to give their prospects. So when the prospects come and drop the coupons, you will be able to know who referred them to you. For ease of use and identification, the coupons could carry specific codes or ID on it. In any case, they are only paid after the prospect makes the purchase; hence, for both side, it's without risk.

Going about the online way, there are various sites you can sign up that will put your offer on their network, such that their followers get to see it. Sites like clickbank.com, amazon.com (in addition, it is a great place to sell), CJ.com, etc. With these sites, access is granted such that you to reach their affiliates through them. Those affiliates sign up and start promoting your offers. Another way is to go about the use of private affiliate programs out there that may be gotten freely or at a quite cheap price to handle your own affiliate programs without the demand for another network.

Essentially, in any route you undertake, do not expect that affiliates will magically sign up and promote your offer without you raising a finger. It takes an effort to reach out and get these affiliates to make them promote your work. In addition, reach out to the people who you can help in return. This guarantees that you have a great money converting offer with good payouts to make your offer very attractive to these affiliates.

Something to run with: Develop an affiliate program and try to get affiliates to help you promote your offers at close to zero risk to you. In addition, make your offers and payouts attractive. Ensure that you intelligently, reach out to the best affiliate prospects available.

30 Use Free Review Copies for Influencers, Like Bloggers, Pinterest Users

Do you have any idea that some big influencer out there online can single-handedly drive millions of dollars in sales, with a single post of your products on social media? Do you know that another group of people can achieve that by mentioning your products on their big blog? In fact, there are businesses that are billion-dollar businesses now that had gotten their start from big influencers mentioning or advertising their products.

Really, it is easier to get these influencers to mention your products than you think. Truly, it may be more difficult to launch from a big star mentioning that your product is nice, but there are still well-known influencers that can make a ton of sales gravitate your way. Who knows, it may just be your lucky day and your product may go viral.

To boost your chances of this, you should try reaching out to these big influencers, blogs, news sites and offer them free samples of your productivity, in hopes that they would be will to give a review or a mention.

More often than not, these influencers demand to be paid before they can mention your product. As much as some of the biggest influencers may cost a serious amount of money, there are others who will do it for just a little amount of money. Consider it: about $100 or so for a minute or two of their time is a very considerate and good deal. Even for some semi-well known influencers, cutting such a deal is enough to get you all the exposure you need.

To locate these influencers, just head on to social media sites—
Facebook, Twitter, Instagram, Pinterest, YouTube and so on. In
addition, they can be found on online forums, blogs, big news sites,
magazines and so on. Reach out to the directly on those sites via direct
messages or their e-mails—which is often in their bio.

Something to run with: Make some research, identify and reach out to
influencers and big sites to see if they would be willing to give your
product a mention, even if it is for a price or write a review of your
products for a free copy of it. Cutting these deals, can create a big boost
in sales for you.

31 Go For the Big Fish Deal

Business owners try to fight over the crumbs. They rush to make deals or land sales with anyone and everyone that they can cut deals with, even if those deals are worth little money to them.

However the change that happens when you try to get bigger clients or choose bigger businesses to cut deals with is amazing. A single deal is more than enough to make for a great business month (or even business year).

There are two main ways of approaching this. First off, you can target more high-end prospects that offer more. Like some prior tips that had been earlier mentioned raising your prices and offering more "ready-made" services and products, you can aim for the elite buyers instead on focusing on going for the low-priced leads. The second way is to focus on big competitors or on other business owner who are more established, far bigger than you in a similar market but not competing with you and then endeavor to strike a deal with them to sell or help promote your offers (for a big cut). Making this hands-free, easy to run and profitable for them, it would shock you how many of them will be willing to cut deals with you.

A way to achieve the second suggestion is by offering to white label your own products and service. White label means to all someone to sell your offer as theirs while you do all the work to provide the services. Eventually, you get a cut and they get a cut too. This can be a win for both sides, as the your focus is to fulfill the sales, do the support and make lots of sales without having to spend any money on advertising or do any marketing by yourself while their own focus is to make good a and easy sales for you and get a great cut in return. A single deal like this can totally establish your business.

Something to run with: Go for the big fish at all times, by going after the elite prospects at higher prices giving them better offers. Another way is to seek out big partnerships to do white label deals, where sales of your offers are made for you at a great cut.

32 Engage Your Clients and Prospects in Discussion Bothering Around What They Want

Getting caught in the desire to make profit, business owners end up doing more talking than listening. However, making sales involves a lot of listening than talking. Rather than spending a lot of time, over-thinking and brain storming about what may please your prospects and your customers, why not just ask them? You would be surprised that it may not be that hard to sell them what they are telling you they need.

For example, if you are selling a wide range of online marketing or web services, instead of forcing your customers or prospect to buy a particular SEO package to help rank their site, why not inquire of them what they think their biggest issues are right now in their business? During the discussion, you may discover that they are not really interested in the ranking but might need help with their social media optimization, email list management or some other services that you could easily provide for them.

Whenever someone tells you the issues they are encountering in their business, try to ask them what they think fixing those issues would do to their business and then ask them how much more they assume they could make if all those problems were fixed and everything was running smoothly. Eventually, they end up telling you the value that those services carry to them. Rather than you trying to convince them of the value that you can bring to the table, just listen to them and talk with them. Stop talking about yourself or your service and just listen to what their needs are, the more you talk about yourself these less likely it is that you would land those sales.

In addition, this method works quite well both for prospects who need to be convinced before they make their first purchase from you and for existing customers that you could sell other things to. For instance, you may find that all of your clients who have been getting a particular service from you, really desire to buy a different service if only you offered it. And it just might be an incredibly easy service for you to either offer or outsource.

Something to run with: Request of your prospects and clients what they need, what would help them and make life more comfortable for them. Listen to their needs, talk a lot less, provide them with a product or service that fulfills the need, sell it to them and make your sales.

33 Outsource Services That You Can Sell Yourself

As much as it is a great idea to add extra services that you sell and provide yourself it is not always practical because there only so much you can do and there's only so much time in a day. Therefore it may be a great idea to look for other activities that you can sell but outsource to other when it comes to doing the actual work—you really get to do little or no work on your end.

For example, you may be a web designer that often gets requests to create a website and add videos to it but it might be time consuming or perhaps impossible for you to create a video that really looks nice enough to sell as a service, even if you could make a high amount per sale for each video made and added.

Instead do just letting such money go, look for people online who offer those services normally, reach out to them, negotiate prices with them and get their permission to use the testimonials, social proof, examples, sales pages, as your own (or modify it to your taste) to sell to your own customers. This is a great option to consider making some extra money and boosting your profit margin.

Take for example, there are online sites and even phone applications like Fiverr.com, Craigslist.com, Freelancer.com etc., that have a massive number of online workers who can do almost anything you need them to. In some cases, you can find workers who can make really nice videos for $25 to $50 (even lesser sometimes) and you could then sell that service for hundred to even thousands of dollars.

Adding some of these services to your own service may not cost a lot and may not demand much work, but why not make a fortune almost doing nothing.

Something to run with: Keep your eyes open for other service or offers that you can sell but get to outsource the real work involved for a little amount. This can boost the money going into your sales funny without adding any extra work or extra working time for you

34 Offer Premium Support Services (White Gloves, Warranties, Free Upgrades, Etc.)

I presume every one of us at one time or the other has bought electronics with an additional warranty. In another case, you may have purchased a furniture and been offered a service called white glove service that involved Delbert and setting up of the new couch.

These examples mentioned above are examples of premium support service that can give very large profit margins, which makes you unperturbed because if only a small percentage of customers subscribe to these services, they can add a lot to your bottom line.

These premium support services can be at little or no cost to you. For instance, one business can be at no cost for you. Take for example, one business gives a warranty offer that provides you with a free replacement charger cables forever on your phone, if they ever fail, for a small token, as long as you just cover the small shipping and handling fee. However, these cables provide such huge profit margins, that the small Shipping and Handling fee covered the cost of the cables and the s Shipping. Obviously the warranty that was sold was a 100% purr profit, despite how it appeared to be a great deal for the buyers. Think about it, paying $5 for shipping and handling for a new cable priced for about $29 is a pretty good deal.

Providing services like offering faster support, faster shipping and delivery, faster services; all of these can give huge margins with little or no extra work.

Something to run with: Considering a couple of extra premium support services that can you can offer your customers—buyers, precisely—that come with huge profit margins despite not increasing your cost of execution.

35 Provide Free Plus Shipping & Handling Products

To get people to take actions, especially online, one of the best things you can do is to offer a free plus shipping and handling offer. Such offers carry obvious huge values because nothing is cheaper than free. By enjoining customers to pay a small Shipping and Handling free, the value of the free product becomes obvious, even though the cost of the free product might be completely covered in the Shipping and Handling fee.

For instance, a site like Aliexpress.com specializes in drop-shipping products of all sorts, you can find lots of jewelry, pet toys, and gadgets and so on, for under $2 which already covers free shipping. However, the values of these goods are perceived to be about $10 to $30 or more.

This translates that your customers get a great deal by assuming that they got the best bargain ever, while you also get a deal by winning a new customer at no cost to you. Let me make it clearer, if the product and shipping cost $2, you are up to a $3 profit by charging $5 Shipping and Handling fee.

Apparently, it is difficult to be very rich at a few bucks at a time, therefore you treat these offers as an access point to note other offers. Hence you would have to offer them, as time progressed, additional up-sell, other products on your back-end and take full advantage of their email addresses to reach out with additional offers later on. From that point on, ensure that every transaction is pure profit for you.

Something to run with: Take an impulse buy product with a free plus shipping and handling offer where you lose your own money after collecting the small charge. After that, up-sell them with your consequent offers to make the most of your money.

36 Try Adding Physical Products as a Bonus, Especially For Your Digital Offers of Services

Dealing in digital products like e-books or videos (even services) can be awesome because they often carry higher profit margins than physical product. Although this is what is obtainable, people place a much higher value in palpable products that can be touched, held and taken around with them.

However, this does not mean that you have to make all your products physical ones. Instead, you should consider offering physical products that are simple, like a branded coffee mug, hat, t-shirt or some other product that make sense with the digital offers or services that you have made available, as a bonus for those who take quick action.

Eventually, you achieve two things. First, it makes people take fast actions because they know that there is a limited quantity of the physical product (while the digital they know that you can have as many as you desire). Secondly, a high value we placed on physical products that can be touched!

Although it may sound crazy, you can boost your conversion on a website service of $2,000 by giving a branded coffee mug or T-shirt as a bonus. Also, it makes it easy to increase conversions on lower priced products where you give away something that they assume to be worth so much or more than what they are purchasing. Take for instance, a newsletter could be sold for $19/month with every new subscriber getting a free T-shirt. In some cases, such offers can double your conversions because it is assumed that the value of the shirt is worth more than the $19 paid. In addition, they may just stay for a longer time and more money may be made from them.

Here is another example, if you sold a phone case for $29 and added a free charging cable to it as a bonus, since many of those cables sell for $29 themselves, the value of the offer is perceived to be huge, although it might only add a dollar or two to your cost and your wide profit margin is still insured.

The same idea can be adopted for services that you offer. For example, you could offer a free cell phone clip-on lens with any custom web video purchased.

For an offline physical product or trial version, a free towel and sweatband could be offered for trying out a one-month gym membership as a trial.

It is shocking how your conversions can skyrocket or leap even for higher priced products and even more shocking is how much they can boost your lower priced offerings.

Something to run with: Physical products should be added as bonuses to your offers as they can tremendously boost conversions for both your low and high-priced products and services.

37 Offer Different Packages/Buying Options to Boost the Perceived Value and Sales (Even With No Intention of Selling the Others)

Most times, it can be a wise idea to offer multiple packages that are quite similar when selling something. However, instead of offering very different packages which might make your prospect hesitant due to not being sure which option to go for, you can provide similar options that seem to have more value such that it is perceived as an amazing deal.

For instance, let us assume that you are selling.an SEO service to help website rank better. If your main offer is a ready-made package for $997 where you help them in ranking their site and offer some basic additional consultations for them too, that can normally seem like a lot of money to some people and can make them more hesitant, stuck on making a decision to buy or not to buy. In another way, you can offer three options where the basic package is for $897 and only includes a diagnosis and report of what the identified issues is but does not include fixing the problem, the "most popular" package is for $997 and includes the service in the basic package and fixing all the issues with an added advantage of three consultation calls and the "elite" package goes for $1,997 and includes everything in the most popular package but also includes unlimited consultation calls for a month.

By smartly calculating, almost everyone assumes that the "most popular" package is the best deal. It appears to be only a little more than the basic packaged but it carries more value. On the other hand, the "elite" package is twice the price but only has some extra consultation calls that most are sure that they may never really need. In a blink, there is a change of perception that the $997 option is cheaper and offers a great deal. For you, the other options are not meant to necessarily get sales. The purpose of those two is simply mean to help accentuate the worth and value of your main offer.

Literally writing something like Basic Package, Most Popular and Elite Package next to the options, you can assist your customers in differentiating between each of the service and gravitate towards the Most Popular One.

Something to run with: In your business, offer multiple packages like a Basic, Most Popular and Elite packages, where the value of the Most Popular one seems huge in comparison to the other in order to make more people move towards it and perceive it as a really great deal.

38 Try Split Testing

Often business owners and marketers will only make one version of an offer, sales page, opt-in page, advertisement available and simple keep their fingers cross. If it works out, they are happy. If it does not, they think that the offer simply is unworkable.

This is a horrible way to go about doing business. If the first attempt does not work out as you hoped, you should look into creating several different versions of the offer or sales copy. To your surprise, it may be that something is not right in your sales copy. Also, even if you were lucky enough to get a winning offer at your first try, you should try to constantly test new things in the sales copy to know if you can increase clicks to your advertisement, lead conversions, opt-in pages, sales to your sales page and up-sells to your up-sell pages.

It might not demand so much hard changes. Just changing headlines around or minute changes can cause the drastic change. For instance, you may discover than changing a headline and cutting down the length of an opt-in page nay boost your lead conversions from 20% to 30%.

That bit of minute change may increase your sales by a staggering 50%. Also by making mild adjustments on your up-sell page, you may find out that you have boosted your conversions from 5% to 8% which would be a 60% increase in the back-end! Minute changes can go a long way and can flip a losing business plan into a winning business plan.

Something to run with: Be adventurous enough to try new things like new sales copy, offers and so on in order to see if you can increase your opt-in rate, sale conversions or up-sell conversions. Minute changes can cause a great effect that can turn your business around.

39. Run Contests

Running contests can be an effective way to get more leads or prospects, get feedback from existing customers, and encourage more people to participate on webinars. You do not need to give away something very expensive like a car. Actually, giving away cheaper things help increase your conversions even more (maybe because they believe with the cheaper stuff they'll have a better chance of winning).

For example, you run advertisement for a contest for a product that you want to sell. Anyone who chooses to come around is probably interested in the product you want to sell. When they approach you, you can advertise, immediately, a special deal you have on that product in case they do not win the contest and desire to still get it right away. Advantageously, you can get cheap clicks and leads when advertising this way on places like Facebook, while building a very good target list of leads.

A contest can also be used as a way to build up testimonials. You could devise a way in which when customers submit any testimonial or feedback about your product, they enter into the contest directly. Contending for a thing and the fact that they can get something for free without paying is why it can be a great way to get customers and potential customers to take action.

Something to run with: Use contest to get lots of traffic on your site, such that more leads tend to check out your offers. Alternatively, use contests to encourage testimonials or feedback on your product. These testimonials could be used for advertisements which draws potential customers—just kill two birds with one stone.

40 Find Prospects in Forums, Q&A sites, Blogs and Social Media That You Can Help

Are you waiting to be located by prospects, why not get off your seat and go find them? One of the ways of doing this is by locating them in forums, Q&A sites like Yahoo Answers and Quora. Social media like Facebook, Twitter, Instagram and blogs may also serve this purpose.

Prospects may be found asking questions relevant to your niche and asking for professional advice on what to go for. By taking a few minutes to give a response on those sites, you are not only helping that one potential prospect out, but you find out that dozens, hundreds or potentially even thousands of people or even more, will eventually apply your response. Those thousands of people may have the same question of their mind so it leads them to check out your site, video or offer. The plan is to ensure to provide value first and foremost; rather than just spamming your link or offer around.

For example if you're dealing in diamonds or are just an affiliate of a diamond site, you can be on the lookout for prospects asking questions on what to look for, if a particular diamond they were about to get is a good deal, what sites are best and the list goes on. When you provide solutions, you can also direct them to your sites or videos where you might have more important information on the question that the prospect just asked, along with your links or affiliate links to your recommended sites or offers. You could even spice it up a little more by offering a free service where you assist in picking out diamonds for them based on the criteria they give. To do that you n need to ask if they need your help, once the answer is positive you could send your

56

recommended links to your offers or affiliated links to your recommended sites as email before you decide to help them.

Interestingly, you can do this on high traffic sites, those sites ranking on Google and other search engines, to make sure that your efforts payoff maximally by giving it a high likelihood to be seen by others.

Something to run with: Set out some time to find places where your prospects hang out online and provide answers to their questions by leading them back to your site, videos or offers.

41. Create a Network of Content and Videos across the Web, Asking and Answering All the Common Questions That Your Prospects Must Have

Out there, online, searching for an answers to their questions are your potential prospects. For instance, if they are in the market to purchase a moped, they are probably searching on Google right now on questions like: what is the difference between a 50cc engine and a 150cc engine? What scooter is the best for carrying two people? What is a moped is all-electric and good? Literally hundreds of common questions are being asked by your prospects that they are searching for relevant answers on.

Although we may have earlier talked about finding people out there asking questions on sites like forums, a number of people would rather not post question but just rub straight to Google to make their research themselves. For this reason, it is expedient that you have lot of content in form of blog posts, webpages, videos, article etc., where you are trying to capture their questions in the title of your posts or video and then proffering last solution within the body of your video.

If you take some time, say about half an hour a week to create some more content and capture a different a different keyword or question in every post, you will find that you will begin to start ranking for keywords and start bringing a lot of traffic your way, your site. It may even drive offers your way (just ensure to recommend specific offers to them through your links or affiliate links at the end). Literally, you will be creating a network of content to catch these prospects, at every level at hurl them towards yourself.

Something to run with: Create content and videos that target questions that your prospects are asking online, answer the questions with finesse and while doing so introduce them offers that may help them with their questions—offers that would wheel them to you.

42 Make proper use of An E-mail Marketing (Better than you used to)

Although e-mail marketing is cheap and highly effective, yet few businesses take advantage of it. E-mail costs fractions of a percentage point of the cost of mailing flyers, postcard; yet, business rarely use it.

Online marketers, who focus on building up email list of customers or prospects to promote their offers, do not actually send mails to their email lists as they ought. Business owners seem to forget that there are tons of competitors online. Competitors are sending e-mails to your leads already whether you like it or not. If you send emails to your list only about 2 or 3 times a month, they most likely will forget who you are. Even if they do not forget you, you are denying yourself a lot of opportunities to mail them concerning offers that you could sell to them, affiliate programs and many more. Mailing a few time times a week or mailing them daily should be considered, especially if you could be marketing more than only one product to them.

In addition, be absolutely certain that you are collecting these leads, building a list and taking complete advantage of e-mail auto responders out there. If not, you're being ignorant, leaving a ton of money to waste away.

Something to run with: building an email list is not enough but you should also mail them too. Try mailing your list about a few times a week, if not daily with several different offers in the mail.

43 Try Optimizing Multiple Keyword on Different Pages of Your Website

Most businesses do not do a great job at targeting keywords on their website. At most, they try to rank for a single keyword but even they do not do a great job at targeting it.

To get lots of organic traffic and ranking well is to choose several keywords (a dozen can be a good start), where each of your pages within your website (or each blog post within your blog) are trying to be optimized for a different keyword.

This can be achieved by having the keywords that you are trying to rank on a particular page or blog post in your title and title tags (title tags are blue links that show up in Google in the search results—your title tags should have rich and appealing keywords). Let's assume that the term you are trying to target is "puppy potty training", you can make that a part of your title while also making it interesting, attractive and appealing like "Puppy Potty Training—5 Minute Trick to Potty Train Your Puppy." This makes you not only target your main keywords but it makes your post more attractive and appealing and will get more traffic which can help boost your rankings.

In addition, you could target other puppy training terns on other pages of your site while ensuring to optimize each and every one of those words. In the same vein, if you are a lawyer trying to rank your business, consider making separate web pages on your website where each on narrows on a particular type of law that you undertake, while intentionally targeting keywords that are related to your profession. For example a page could be regretting "Immigration Lawyer in Atlanta,

GA" while another page could be targeting "Real Estate Attorney in Atlanta, GA" and so on.

Providing keywords and title tags is not enough. Consideration should be given to optimizing other aspects of your website like the description tags (the text below the blue link that appear in the search result of Google), schemas (information supplied to search engines to rank you better and show more information about you) and site maps (a table of content from your website). If you have no idea what these things mean, no worries; there are tools that are used to fix these issues like WebFire.com that can help you in the optimization of your website and also help to fix all these issues for you. In addition, they are also equipped to fix other issues like helping you find leads, create and distribute content, analyze keywords)

Something to run with: Pick a variety of keywords, related to the website you own. Use specific keywords on specific pages of your website to give you the most probable chance of ranking for each search engine.

44 Use the Language of Your Consumers

Owners of businesses often get caught up in their own language. More than they know, they forget that their consumers do not understand a lot of the technical terms that they use.

To get around these little problem, business owners may need to dial down on the business jargon in their sales copy and advertising materials. Even more, during general sales conversations, try to use the everyday language of the people that you are trying to attract. For example, although a lot of people know that SEO is an acronym for Search Engine Optimization and it is a way to help your website rank better, the population who may be in need your SEO service do not know what any of that means! Rather than typing "SEO services" or "SEO tools" on Google, they are most definitely typing with terms like "rank on Google tools" or "getting better rankings" or "how to appear on the first page of Google" instead.

Dialing down the language in terms of ranking is not the only consideration. When it comes to communicating with your consumers whom you are trying to target, it is important to dial down the language used in your sales messages as well into the everyday language of the consumers. This will not only make them able relate with you but it also increases the likelihood of them coming to purchase from you because they are buying what they understand.

Something to run with: Try dialing down the technical language used in your sales messages. Ensure to speak in the everyday language of your target market not the technical terms only understood by fellow business owners.

45 Be Big and Bold In Your Advertisement and Sales Copy

In business, being mediocre or boring does not get you anywhere. In a world where people are bombarded with advertisements and other offers all the time, you need to have something that stands out. One way to achieve this is to make sure that on your advertising messages, you are big and bold.

For instance, if you are selling a course on how to learn piano easily, do not put up an advertisement that days something like, "learn how to play the piano easily". Such a statement will simply get overlooked amidst the competition. However, a phrase like, "Learn how to play the piano like a pro in 7 days or less!"

Consider another example, instead of selling a weight loss course with a redundant headline like, "Five ways to lose weight", how about "Five breakthrough easy weight loss technique to lose 10 pounds in a week with minimal effort". As much as you want the statement to be true, if you do not spice up your advertising and sales copy by making big and bold statements, you may just get lost in the mist of other advertisements and you will not get the attention of your prospects.

Something to run with: Make a big and bold statement in your advertisement that focuses on the results or benefits in an attractive way that makes you unique from the other competitors. In place of an advertisement that says, "Learn to play the piano easily," go for something more eye-catching like, "Learn how to play the piano like a pro in 7 days or less!"

46 Know Your Statistics, Numbers and Data

Do you have an idea what the lifetime value of your customers is? Do you have an idea what it costs you to acquire customers? Do you have an average idea of how many of your customers stay? How frequently do you convert a lead to actual sales? How long does it take to make this conversion? What is the worth of your up-sell and back-end for each front-end sale? What is the average worth of your lead to you and what does it costs to you to acquire the lead?

Above are necessary questions that you should ask answers to as a business owner. However, if you cannot give an answer to these questions, there is a probability that you have been losing a lot of money by not knowing these figures. As a business owner, it is necessary to know points in your business where you need to improve. However if you have no idea the area of your business that needs true improvement, you are shooting blindly and hoping to luckily hit your target.

Quite often, the difference between a great and workable business plan and a bad one is just having good knowledge of what the figures say and the true value of your customers. Consider that you were spending $10 to acquire a $5 customer from day one. What would your response be? Reasonably, most people would abandon such a business plan and assumed that it has failed. However, if you knew your figures and knew that on average, you make $15 more on every customer on the back-end within the first three months, you would not toss out a campaign that would double your money.

Consider this: if you just observed the end results and saw that you were making $12 on every $10 spent, so you decided to boost your advertisement to get richer $2 dollars at a time. However, you fail to realize that you have a great front-end conversion but terrible upsell conversion (or horrible opt-in rates but great sales conversions). Diligently studying and fixing the area that is wrong might be able to push that $12 into $25. Hence you are richer much faster!

Having a good idea of where the areas of your problems are tells you what to fix and how to fix it much faster. Therefore understanding your number and data makes the creation and growth of a business much easier and progresses geometrically.

Something to run with: Put more efforts into knowing your number and data. Gather information like your conversion rates, lifetime values of your customers etc., so you can get the full picture of your business and what is required to grow faster and more profitably.

47 The Price that A Customer Sees First Can Discourage or Encourage A Customer to Make A Purchase

People's mindset can be easily influenced by several factors. In business, one of those factors is how they perceive the price of a product.

For example, if a person wants to buy a car and has a budget of $15,000, if he sees a preferred car for $30,000, it is unlikely that the person would make such a purchase because it is above his budget. Even if he sees a car for $20,000 the likelihood that he would make the purchase is quite low.

However, if there is a car for $30,000 marked down to $20,000 through a special promotional offer, he'll be likely to spend more than that $15,000 budget because it seems he is getting a great deal for only a little more (he is saving $10,000 for spending $5,000 more).

Consider this other example: imagine that you are planning on adding a stone retaining wall to your house with a budget of $7,000. Let us assume that the contractor comes and says it can only be done for $10,000, you will likely pass or wait until you get another person who will do it for the amount within your budget. Let's imagine if the contractor had said, "Normally, a wall like what you desire would cost you $18,000 to $20,000 depending on the kind of stone used. However, if you are interested in using a particular type of stone on sale this week and can wait till next week when I am free to do it, I can do it for $10,000." Such an offer would make you, the customer, think you are getting a crazy good deal because you get to save nearly $8,000 to $10,000 less than the normal, also you are not really losing anything by using a particular type of stone; as long as it looks like the style you want. Even if it's a few grand more than your budget, you most definitely, will find yourself walk away to look for a means to get the added cash because you think you might be losing a great deal.

Something to run with: The first price that a customer sees, largely influences what type of deal they think you are offering them. Therefore make sure to have a compromise where the price is way more than their budget. However, for just a bit more, they get to make huge saving in comparison to how much more they would have to pay. For instance, if they have a budget of $5,000, do not show a product $7,000 first. Instead, show a product of $12,000 first that is on sale for $7,000 for a limited time. Such a client will count himself or herself fortunate!

48 How You Label People, Determines How They Would Act

Unknowingly, people act based on how they are labeled. If an elderly person is praised for appearing strong, the possibility that he will perform better at a strength test is high. Likewise, if the same elderly person is treated as weak, they will likely not perform very well at a strength test; despite the fact that the elderly person is of the same exact strength in both cases! Therefore this reveals that how a person is labeled, largely defines to what expectations they will perform.

Apply this to your marketing, label your prospects in such a way that it creates hope in them that your product is the perfect solution for them. Take for example, if you sell a course on how to improve your tennis playing skills, instead of acting or communicating to the prospects that they are terrible at the game and they need you, say things like, "just by making the decision to improve your game, your mind is in a place that puts you 95% ahead of other players. All that is required now is to channel your mind into the game. Also, you may need to learn a fee simple shot techniques to make your playing better. From there on, just keep getting better to become the best!" Presenting yourself like this, you're helping them believe in themselves. Also, you make them believe that they are mentally ahead of other and have a potential to be great at the game. Being persuaded enough by your words, they may just decide to take your classes.

Consider another example, if you sell a course on investing, try not to act like you're the only genius in the room and everyone else is an idiot. Instead, tell your prospects that by just being present to learn a few basic that you are above to cover, they will be smarter than 99% of other out there who know nothing about investing. Push further by telling your prospects that they are ahead of the world at the investing game; however, they can take it to the next level by grabbing your course.

Something to run with: The ways you label your prospects can affects and influence the actions they take and their performance. Having the knowledge of this, use the knowledge to your advantage by making them feel smart because they examined your offer. You could also tell them how smart they are but just a few modifications away from being awesome!

49. For Higher Priced Offers, Try Webinars

In case webinars seems new to you, it is simply where you go on a—mostly live—video call to watch the presentation of a product. There you can see the presenter of the product and hear their voice. In the marketing world, this platform is used as a means of giving out some content and then persuading you—the prospect—to try to buy the product or offer.

There usually is a registration page where the prospects enter their e-mail addresses and then proceed to the live call. In most cases, a portion of the people who visit hardly registers, therefore if you can get half to register that is good. In addition, if your presentation is persuading enough to get a third of those registered to show up in person, then that is great; because persuading people enough to show up is serious work. However, those that show up are very likely to buy from you after watching your presentation.

Advisably, webinars should be employed to sell offers that are higher priced that cannot fit in for impulse buys. Products priced from $500 to thousands of dollars do well on webinars because the conversion rates are, most times, lot higher compared to a sales page or video sales page. Therefore, if you possess a sales page that is not doing as great as you hoped, consider giving webinar a try. Another tip is this: if you have a low-priced offer that is not doing quite well, just raise the price and add more value to the offer, then try selling it on webinar. The results may shock you!

Something to run with: For higher priced offers that do not fall within the range of impulse buys, try using webinars to sells them. On these ones, conversion rates can be much higher.

50. Use Incentives to Get More Likes, Shares and Promote Your Content/Offers

If you content on social media, website or blog is great, take advantage of it by employing the use of incentives to make your readers like, share, and promote your content, offer or product. To get this done, you do not need to offer much in return. As small an act as just mentioning that your reader should like or help share your content for a chance to win a prize may increase your shares, traffic and rankings. This method works regardless if it is a post on social media, a website or a YouTube video.

For example, if you do reviews of video games and the console itself on YouTube; to encourage growth, you can request of your viewers to subscribe to get updates on new video game content; to like and comment in the section below for a chance to win a Gift Card of $50 to some known gaming sites, a game, some gaming equipment, or whatever the game lovers that follow you may like. Shockingly, people may take serious advantage of this and this can help boost your rankings, ability to get traffic on your site that easily and visibility

Also, if you had a Facebook post or blog post that was related to your gardening product, you could tell your viewers to share and comment for an opportunity to win your gardening product for no price. Requesting for likes, comments and shares, without an incentive, can boost the chances of getting it done. However, by using incentives to encourage them, you may achieve more.

Something to run with: Try using incentives on your readers to get likes, shares, comments, subscriptions etc., on your social media posts, blog posts and videos to boost the traffic, rankings and exposure to your content.

Conclusion

Hopefully, you discovered a number of handful tips that you may decide to act on. Do not belabor yourself with the thought of implementing these tips perfectly. Most times, taking quick actions will get you better results than trying to make the perfect move.

Also, do not underestimate the drastic effect that any one or two of these tip can cause in your business. Personally implementing some of these tips in the past had huge productive effects on our businesses; even though these tips didn't request so much.

Actually, applying one or two of these tips can make your business better or worse. Therefore, select a few of your favorite tips and begin to take actions on them this week! Taking actions is the difference between the successful people and the unsuccessful ones.

To Learn More

http://oriontrainingportal.com

http://mrplr.co.education

http://trainingacademyportal.com

http://making-money-athome.com

http://lulu.com/spotlight/Tomkhatt